Note to Parents and Teachers

The SCIENCE STARTERS series introduces key science vocabulary and concepts to young children while encouraging them to discover and understand the world around them. The series works as a set of graded readers in three levels.

LEVEL 3: READ ALONE
These books can be read alone or as part of guided or group reading. Each book has three sections:

• Information pages that introduce key concepts. Key words appear in bold for easy recognition on pages where the related science concepts are explained.
• A lively story that recalls this vocabulary and encourages children to use these words when they talk and write.
• A quiz asks children to look back and recall what they have read.

ANIMALS IN DANGER looks at CONSERVATION. Below are some answers and activities related to the questions on the information spreads that parents, carers, and teachers can use to discuss and develop further ideas and concepts:

p. 7 *What do you think will happen to pandas if all the bamboo forests are cut down?* Like all animals, pandas cannot survive in the wild away from the natural habitats where they have the food, water, and shelter they need. When we cut down a forest, we are destroying the homes of thousands of different animals, from minibeasts such as insects and snails, to bigger animals such as birds, reptiles, and mammals.

p. 9 *Should people buy things made from animals in danger?* No. Buying things made from parts of endangered animals encourages hunters to go on killing them.

p. 11 *What other animals do you think oil spills harm?* Oil spills hurt all kinds of sea animals, especially those who come to the surface of the water, such as seals, otters, killer whales, and penguins. They can also affect seaweed, clams, oysters, and mussels.

p. 13 *What is happening in your area that puts animals in danger?* Take children on a nature walk and encourage them to notice what wild creatures are around them and which trees and plants they use. Then, for example, when they see a buddleia bush being cut down, they will appreciate its loss as a source of food for butterflies and other insects.

p. 19 *Ask your teacher whether your class or school can sponsor an animal in danger, such as a gorilla, tiger, or dolphin.* Many local parks or zoos with breeding programs run animal sponsor schemes. National and worldwide organizations include: wwf.org, www.wildlifeaid.org, www.caww.com, www.pawsweb.org.

ADVISORY TEAM

Educational Consultant
Andrea Bright—Science Coordinator, Trafalgar Junior School

Literacy Consultant
Jackie Holderness—former Senior Lecturer in Primary Education, Westminster Institute, Oxford Brookes University

Series Consultants
Anne Fussell—Early Years Teacher and University Tutor, Westminster Institute, Oxford Brookes University

David Fussell—C.Chem., FRSC

CONTENTS

© Aladdin Books Ltd 2008

Designed and produced by
Aladdin Books Ltd

First published in
the United States in 2008 by
Stargazer Books
c/o The Creative Company
123 South Broad Street
P.O. Box 227, Mankato,
Minnesota 56002

Printed in the United States
All rights reserved

Editor: Sally Hewitt
Designer: Jim Pipe
Series Design: Flick, Book
Design & Graphics

Thanks to:
The pupils of Trafalgar
Infants School for appearing
as models in this book.

**Library of Congress
Cataloging-in-Publication Data**

Pipe, Jim, 1966-
  Conservation / by Jim Pipe.
    p. cm. -- (Science starters)
  ISBN 978-1-59604-136-3
  (alk. paper)
  1. Wildlife conservation--
Juvenile literature. I. Title.

QL83.P57 2007
333.95'416--dc22

                2007009205
2-2012 PO1457

Photocredits:
*l-left, r-right, b-bottom, t-top,
c-center, m-middle*
Cover tl & tc, 4 both, 5bl, 8bl, 9tr,
10b, 14tr, 21b, 28tr, 31bl—Corbis.
Cover tr & b, 2tl, 7b, 10b, 12b,
14b, 15t & bl, 16 both, 17tl, 18b,
19tr, 22b, 26t, 27 both, 28bl, 29bl,
30, 31br & 31bcl, 11bl & br—
istockphoto.com. 2bl, 7tr, 13br,
20tr—Comstock. 2ml, 3, 5br, 6
both, 11tr, 17br, 20b, 21tr, 29m,
31tr, ml & mr—Digital Vision. 5tl
& tr, 13tr—Photodisc. 8tr, 24bl,
31bcl—John Foxx Photos. 10tr,
18tr, 19bl, 24tr, 25 all, 26br, 29tr
—Marc Arundale / Select Pictures.
12tr, 13ml, 15mr—Stockbyte. 17tr
—Ingram Publishing.

SCIENCE STARTERS

LEVEL

3

CONSERVATION

Animals in Danger

by Jim Pipe

Stargazer Books

ANIMALS IN DANGER

Tiger

There are millions of different animals around the world. Some of these animals are in **danger**, like this tiger.

Whale

There are just a few hundred tigers left in the world. They could die out. When they are gone, they are gone forever.

You may know some other big animals that are in **danger**, like whales and rhinoceroses.

Many small animals are in **danger** too, such as frogs and butterflies.

But why are all these animals in **danger**?

Cutting Down Forests
When people destroy animal homes, they have nowhere to live.

Hunting
When people kill too many animals, they can destroy them forever.

Getting Warmer
Earth is getting warmer. This is making life hard for animals like polar bears.

Pollution
People poison animals when they put chemicals into the water or soil.

DESTROYING HABITATS

Wild animals need a home where they can live and eat. We call this their **habitat**.

Orangutans are in danger because people are cutting down the forests where they live.

Cutting down trees destroys the orangutans' **habitat**. Soon, they will have nowhere to live.

Orangutan

Trees make a good **habitat** for animals all over the world.

We can help animals by planting trees. A tree in your backyard will be a home for birds, insects, and squirrels.

Planting a tree

Panda

A panda mostly eats bamboo. It needs to live in a bamboo forest.

What do you think will happen to pandas if all the bamboo forests are cut down?

7

HUNTING AND PETS

Some animals are in danger because people **hunt** too many of them.

In Africa, rhinoceroses are **hunted** for their horns.

Rhinoceroses could die out because so many have been killed.

Rhinoceros

Cheetahs

Other animals are also in danger from human **hunters**.

Whales are **hunted** for their meat. Cheetahs are **hunted** for their fur.

8

Some objects are made from parts of animals that are in danger.

Ivory comes from elephant tusks. Shells and coral come from sea animals. Should people buy things made from animals in danger?

Every year, many macaws are taken from the forest. They are sent to other countries where people keep them as **pets.**

Macaws do not make good **pets.** They should live in a forest.

Macaw

LITTER AND POLLUTION

When you drop **litter**, it can harm animals. Birds can get caught up in plastic trash.

To a baby seal, a plastic bag looks like a jellyfish. Eating the bag can kill it. When you pick up **litter**, you could save an animal's life.

Picking up litter

Baby seals

If you pour some oil into a bowl of water, the oil floats on the surface.

When oil spills from a big tanker, it poisons sea birds. What other animals do you think it harms?

Farmers use strong chemicals to stop bugs eating their plants. These chemicals hurt many insects.

When chemicals flow into a lake, they poison the fish. We call this **pollution**. An otter that eats these fish will be poisoned too.

Otter

Not all farmers use chemicals. Some use ladybugs, which eat pests such as aphids.

PROTECTING WILDLIFE

All living things need each
other to live, even humans.
Plants provide food for animals.
Animals also help plants.

Worms make soil good
for growing plants. Birds,
bees, and butterflies carry
pollen from flower to flower.

We should look after,
or **protect**, all **wildlife**.

Animals make
our world a
beautiful place!

Butterfly

Big and small animals need **protecting**. If a small animal dies out, there is no food for the bigger animals that eat it.

When chemicals kill the insects in a field, there is less food for birds.

If we take too many fish from the sea, there is no food for penguins and other animals.

Robin

What is happening in your area that puts animals in danger?

Perhaps a wood is being cut down to make a new road? Maybe new houses are being built on farmland?

WILDLIFE PARKS

In some countries, animals are given a safe place to live in. These **parks** are protected. No one may hunt or build houses here.

People visit the **parks** on safaris, but they cannot disturb the animals. Their money pays for the **park**.

Safari

In the past, wolves were shot by human hunters. Now they are protected in some mountain parks.

Turtle

In some places, you cannot go on the beach during the summer. This allows turtles to lay their eggs in safety.

When the baby turtles hatch, they crawl across the beach to the sea.

These coral reefs are in a sea park. Divers are not allowed to hunt sea animals or take coral.

It is hard for some animals to live in cities.

To help, you can put up boxes for birds, bats, or bugs to live in.

ANIMAL RESCUE

Some zoos provide a **safe** home for wild animals while they are growing up.

When it is an adult, this baby tamarin will be put back into the rainforest.

Animal **rescuers** also feed injured animals until they can feed themselves.

Baby tamarin

Feeding a wild mouse

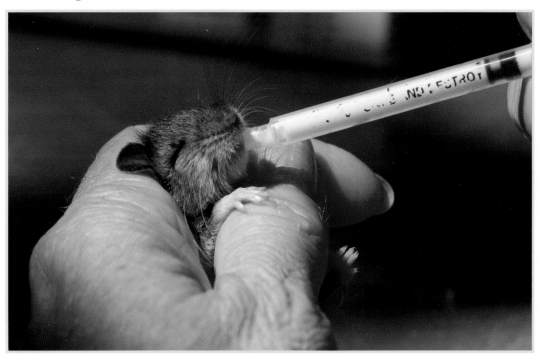

Warning sign

Kangaroo

Roads are dangerous for animals like woodchucks, deer, and kangaroos. Cars often run over them.

Warning signs tell drivers to watch out. Some roads have tunnels under them to help small animals such as toads cross **safely**.

Sometimes, fires drive animals from their homes.

Rescuers look after animals that are hurt in the fire. When the animals are better, they are taken to a safe part of the forest.

17

CONSERVATION

Helping wildlife is called **conservation**.
What can you do to help?

Ecogarden

If you have a garden at school, you can give animals a place to live.

Plant wildflowers to attract insects. A log pile gives insects shelter. A pond is a home for all fish, frogs, and insects.

Put out food and water for birds. You can also feed wildlife by growing plants with berries.

Waxwing eating a berry

The more you know about animals,
the more you can help **conserve** them.
Why not explore wildlife in your area?

Go on a night
walk with an
adult to help you.
Listen out for
animals that are
busy at night.

Take a flashlight.
You might
spot night
hunters such
as foxes, owls,
or raccoons.

Raccoon

Ask your teacher whether
your class or school can
sponsor an animal in
danger, such as a
gorilla, tiger, or dolphin.

SAVING WATER AND ENERGY

There are other ways
you can help wildlife.

Pick up litter when you walk.
You could help clean up
a local beach or pond.

Ask your family or school not
to use chemicals on plants.
These can poison local animals.

Cleaning a pond

If we use less
water, there is
more fresh
water for
wildlife in local
rivers and lakes.

Power plants and cars pollute the air. This pollution is making the world warmer.

This is making life hard for many animals. Polar bears cannot find food because the ice they live on is melting.

When we **save energy**, we create less pollution, so we help wildlife too.

Power plant

Polar bears

EXTINCT ANIMALS

If we do not help animals in danger, they may die out. When an animal dies out, we say it is **extinct**.

Lots of amazing animals are **extinct**. The dinosaurs died out 65 million years ago. There are no dinosaurs alive today.

Woolly mammoths died out 10,000 years ago.

Raptor

Dodo

Birds called dodos are **extinct**.

Dodos used to live on an island in the Indian Ocean. Sailors hunted the dodos for food.

The sailors also brought dogs and cats to the island. These ate the dodos' eggs. Eventually, no dodos were left alive.

Humans have helped many animals to become extinct.

The Tasmanian wolf was wiped out by human hunters 60 years ago.

Find out what you can about these three animals, which are in danger of becoming extinct: the monk seal, panda, and tiger.

Tasmanian wolf

OUR WILDLIFE PARK

Look out for ideas about conservation.

Charlie and Emma were reading about dinosaurs. "What does 'Dinosaurs are extinct' mean?" Charlie asked.

"It means there are no more dinosaurs left alive," said Dad.

"What other animals are extinct?" asked Charlie.

"My teacher said tigers could be extinct soon if we do not help them," said Emma.

"What can we do to help?" asked Charlie.

"Our yard isn't big enough for a tiger!" said Mom. "But we can help local animals like birds."

24

"Let's do something,"
said Emma.
"We can make our very
own wildlife park!"
said Charlie.

"I'll write a list of what we need to do," said Emma.

"Birds need food," said Charlie. "We could put out
nuts and seeds."
"Great idea," said Mom.
"Let's take a look at the yard."

The backyard was a mess. "Let's
pick up the litter," said Dad.
"Birds and other animals
get caught in plastic bags."

"What about the dead leaves?"
asked Charlie.

"Sweep them into a pile under
that bush," said Dad.
"They'll be a home for small
animals in winter!"

There were weeds everywhere.
"Let's dig them up," said Emma.
"Hang on," said Dad. "We can
let this area grow wild. It's a
good home for insects."

"Nettles are food for
caterpillars," said Mom.
"And caterpillars are food
for birds!" said Charlie.

"We could also plant a blackberry bush for the birds," said Mom. "Birds love to eat berries."

"What else do birds need?" asked Charlie. "Water to drink!" said Emma, writing it down on her list.

"Yes," said Mom. "They also like a bath to clean their feathers."

"We can't put a bathtub in the backyard!" giggled Charlie.

"Birds are small," said Dad. "They just need a small pool of water."

Suddenly, Charlie jumped.
"There's something stripy moving in the grass," he shouted.

"It's the neighbor's cat," laughed Emma. "Not a tiger!"

"Won't it hunt our birds?" asked Charlie.

"Yes," said Mom. "But we can make a high tabl for them to feed safely."

"I'll make a birdhouse, too," said Dad. "That will be a safe home for the chicks."

"We need to put it up high so the cat can't reach it," said Charlie.

Over the next few weeks, Mom and Dad helped
Emma and Charlie create a wildlife park.

Dad built a bird table
on top of a tall post.

Charlie and Emma put
nuts into the bird feeder
and water into the birdbath.

That summer, the yard really was a wildlife park!
Birds flew down to feed on the nuts and berries.

Bees and butterflies flew
above the long grass.
One night, Dad even saw
a fox in the backyard.

Emma and Charlie loved their backyard. They took their friends on a wildlife safari!

"I wish I had a wildlife park like this," said May.
"Me too," said Steve.

"Maybe we could ask our teacher to help us make one at school," said Emma. "Then we'll have two wildlife parks to enjoy!"
"So will the birds!" said Charlie.

WRITE YOUR OWN STORY about helping animals. Like Emma, you could also write down a list of all the ways you could help one kind of animal.

What birds need	How I can help
Shelter	Put up a birdhouse
Food	Put out nuts, grow blackberries
Water	Make a birdbath
A Safe Home	Make sure feeding table, birdbath, and birdhouse are high off the ground
A Clean Place to Live in	Don't use chemicals in the backyard

QUIZ

How does cutting down trees in a rainforest put **danger**?

Answer on page 6

What happens to sea **animals** when oil spills from a ship?

Answer on page 11

How could you help wild **animals** in your area?

Answer on page 18, 20, 21

Can you remember why these animals are in danger?

Answers on page 7, 8, 9, 21

INDEX